D0866675

FAMINE

BY RHODA BLUMBERG

FAMINE

FRANKLIN WATTS
NEW YORK | LONDON | 1978
AN !MPACT BOOK

Photographs courtesy of: Food and Agriculture
Organization: pp. 4, 31, 34, 43, 62; United Nations:
pp. 6, (ILO) 16, 28, 35, 58, 71; Agency for International Development: pp. 23, 24, 27, 32, 40, 56,
68; The Rockefeller Foundation: p. 49; Italian Council for Research, issued by FAO: p. 53.

Library of Congress Cataloging in Publication Data

Blumberg, Rhoda.
    Famine.

    (An Impact book)
    Bibliography: p.
    Includes index.
    SUMMARY: Discusses famine, its causes, how
new technology can be applied to food production,
and how people throughout the world can co-
operate to alleviate starvation.
    1. Famines—Juvenile literature.   2. Food
supply—Juvenile literature.   [1. Famines.   2.
Food supply] I. Title.
HC79.F3B56   338.1'9   78-6837
ISBN 0-531-02201-3

CONTENTS

TO JERRY
for wonderful reasons

FAMINE

THE THREAT OF FAMINE

1

"There will be no coming together of minds until a major famine brings people together."

Norman Borlaug, scientist

Can the world feed its people? Our planet may be headed for the largest mass starvation in its history. The number of babies born each year increases alarmingly. Unless population stops growing and food production starts increasing, famines could kill millions.

Unlike an earthquake, a famine is not a sudden disaster. It is a horror that grows slowly, killing the poorest and weakest first. Droughts, floods, typhoons, plant diseases, and insect plagues cause famines.

People can also cause famines. In wartime, armies may destroy crops or take most of the food for themselves. They set up sieges and blockades to deliberately starve an enemy. Revolutions and civil disorders that interfere with trade, farming, and transportation cause famines. The twentieth century has created new threats: worldwide famine from food contamination, radiation, and pollution.

[2]

People never fully recover from famine. Survivors are crippled, blinded, or mentally retarded from prolonged lack of food. Once a famine begins it can last for years, even after the original cause has disappeared. Seeds that should be saved for future crops are often eaten by the starving, and animals that should have been used for breeding are butchered for food before they reproduce. The word "famine" means mass starvation affecting large populations in a large area. Thousands, even millions, die.

TOO MANY PEOPLE

The world is cursed with a problem that grows as the number of people grows. The earth's population was 2,000,000,000 in 1930. It doubled in 45 years, to 4,000,000,000 by 1975. If it continues to grow at its present rate, world population will double again in 35 years. In the first million years of civilization our population rose to 4,000,000,000 people; in the next 35 years it may rise to 8,000,000,000. Try to imagine twice as many people as there are now on our planet by the beginning of the twenty-first century!

In many countries hunger is a normal condition. According to United Nations estimates, nearly 500 million people in the world don't have enough to eat. Ten to 20 million die every year of diseases due to malnutrition. Most of them live in "less developed countries" (LDCs), also called "underdeveloped," or "developing"—mild terms meaning *poorer countries.* Many of them exist on the brink of starvation. Crop failure could push them over the brink from hunger to famine.

The worst part is that most babies are born in the poorer countries. The populations of these countries increase much faster than the populations of richer nations. Some experts estimate that at least five out of six

[3]

babies born each day are born in countries at the bottom of the economic ladder in Asia, Africa, and Latin America.

Bangladesh, for example, one of the world's poorest and most crowded countries, has 83 million people living in an area only 10 percent larger than England. Thousands must beg for food. Within twenty-three years Bangladesh may have twice the number of mouths to feed. Even if the amount of food could be doubled in that time, people would still live a pitiful, hand-to-mouth struggle for survival.

When populations are doubled regularly, results can be staggering. At the present world rate of increase, there could be one person for every square foot of space on our planet in less than seven hundred years; in twelve hundred years, *its inhabitants would weigh more than the earth itself.*

> "A population growing without restraint will double its size every few decades. Before long, the number of people in the world will overtake the available food supply . . . and premature death will visit the human race."

This was written in 1798 by Reverend Thomas Malthus in his *Essay on the Principle of Population as it Affects the Future Improvement of Society.* At a time when large families were looked upon as a source of health, wealth, and happiness, Malthus horrified readers by his chilling statements. According to him, human beings were condemned to a losing race; crops of babies grow faster than crops of food.

**People outside this West African
sports arena already know
what overcrowding is like.**

[5]

The mild-mannered reverend was a doomsday prophet who believed that only great disasters could control population growth, that "premature death must in some shape visit the human race." After epidemics and wars have killed millions, famine destroys the additional overabundance of people. Famine "with one mighty blow, levels the population with the food of the world." Pestilence, war, and famine are nature's ways of guaranteeing that at least some would survive.

Malthus was caricatured, criticized, and condemned in his time. Today, although many scholars reject his theories, some believe that his basic ideas were correct. For instance, Dr. John Knowles, president of the Rockefeller Foundation, said, "We will see increasing famine, pestilence, and extermination of large numbers of people. Malthus has already been proved correct."

A high birthrate is not the only reason for a runaway population. There are more people when the deathrate goes down. Malthus could not foresee that the miraculous advances of medicine would cause deathrates to drop dramatically—making the population problem even worse than he had predicted. In the richer countries people now live almost twice as long as they did in the eighteenth century.

Even in the poorer countries the deathrate has dropped, especially since World War II. In 1946, for example, twenty out of every thousand died each year in Sri Lanka. Improved sanitation and public health cut this annual rate to eight per thousand. Because of modern medicine five times as many infants survive their first year. It's a blessing, but it adds to the population problem.

In this small space in Bangladesh, 36,000 people live as refugees.

[7]

Since the 1960s the birthrate has been decreasing in some of the richer industrial nations, like East Germany, West Germany, Austria, and Britain. By 1976 population growth had stopped completely in these countries. They had reached *zero population growth,* meaning that the number of births each year equals the number of deaths. Birthrates are down by almost half in Western Europe and by a third in North America. Birth control has put the brakes on runaway population growth in many parts of the world.

However, birth control is against the law in many countries. Some nations argue that a large population means economic and political power through bigger armies and more workers. At the World Population Conference in Bucharest in 1974, many poorer nations claimed that birth control was a racist plot by North Americans and Western Europeans to keep them weak and powerless.

Some religions like Catholicism and Islamism oppose birth control. Children are considered gifts from God. In parts of Asia and Africa a man is permitted to have several wives. Among Moslems four wives are allowed, and each woman is expected to show her worth by bearing many children.

Poor people frequently take comfort in large families. They resist any efforts to deprive them of this joy. In addition, they need children in order to survive. Children tend animals, work in the fields, and help crafts people, even when they are only four or five years old. Each extra mouth to feed means two extra hands to work. Grown children are a kind of "social security." When parents grow old and are too feeble to work, their sons and daughters can give them enough to eat. Since the deathrate is still high in many poor countries, couples try to have as many children

[8]

as they can, hoping at least a few will survive to maturity.

The United Nations predicts that more than 90 percent of the increase in population expected by the year 2000 will come from the poorer nations. The worldwide picture is terrifying. We seem to be racing toward disaster.

TOO MUCH WASTE

"Too many people" is just part of the problem. Food supplies are shrinking for another reason. People in the richer countries are eating too much. *Affluence* has been cited as a cause of the world hunger. As people make more money they demand more luxury foods, like beef and pork. They have been eating in quantities far beyond their bodies' needs.

At least one-third of the world's grain is fed to livestock. Livestock in the United States eat more grain than do all the people of India. Why should cattle eat better than human beings?

The United States of America is the world's largest producer and the largest consumer. Its average citizen uses nearly 2,000 pounds (909 kg) of grain a year. Most of this is fed to chickens, hogs, and cattle. Only about 200 pounds (91 kg) of grain are eaten directly in the form of bread and cereal, and about 35 pounds (16 kg) are used each year in the form of beer and whiskey. Today Americans eat twice as much as they did in 1950.

Instead of tightening our belts to make our waistlines smaller, many of us spend money on diet programs and exercise classes. And we have doctor bills to pay because we eat so much that we develop high blood pressure and heart disease.

Most people in richer countries eat twice as much as they should. And we are all wasteful. An Indian, Algerian, or Colombian family could live on what the average American throws into the garbage pail.

In our world of spaceships and satellites, abundance and scarcity exist side by side. Even in rich nations millions of human beings suffer from hunger. Some have to eat pet foods for their meals. They get meat that way! People are dying of hunger, particularly in Latin America, Central Africa, and Asia.

Many people feel that we have a moral duty to cut down on the amount of meat we eat. If we ate less meat we could stop someone else's hunger pangs. But even if we did, the world would still not have enough food to prevent mass starvation. Will our earth be cursed with famines in the future, as it has in the past?

FAMINES
IN THE PAST

**"If God were to appear
before a starving man
he dare take no
other form than food."**

Asian Proverb

Famines in the past were looked upon as normal calamities, part of the cycle of existence. They took place so frequently that people regarded them as disasters that could not be avoided.

The world's oldest written account of famine describes people starving because the Nile failed to overflow and irrigate the land. That account was found on the tomb of Egypt's pharaoh Tosothrus, who lived more than five thousand years ago. After heavy summer rains the Nile used to spill over and enrich the soil along its banks. A wealth of crops grew only when the river's annual overflow irrigated the ground. Whenever the Nile failed to flood, Egyptians starved.

Vast deserts and hostile jungles made Africa a continent that just couldn't grow enough food for all its people. Because most of Africa was an unexplored mystery to Europeans until the nineteenth century, we know little about its famines.

[12]

There are no records of mass starvations in North and South America and, although regional famines have taken place in South America, there hasn't been a large famine in the Western Hemisphere since Columbus's time.

However, catalogues have been compiled listing thousands of famines in China, India, and Europe.

CHINA

China was known as "the land of famine." Droughts, floods, and locust plagues afflicted the country. Even when there was no natural disaster, Chinese peasants barely ate enough to keep alive. "Have you eaten?" was the polite way friends greeted each other. According to a study made at the University of Nanking, famines occurred in China nearly every year between 108 B.C. and 1911. About 45 million Chinese starved to death during the first part of the nineteenth century.

A three-year drought starting in 1876 caused one of history's worst famines. Between 9 and 13 million people died. Attempts to supply food failed. Although granaries were full in many areas, there were only a few narrow mountain roads for transporting grain, and these roads were clogged with the bodies of dead people. Camels, oxen, and mules sent in with supplies were killed and eaten by shrivelled, shrieking mobs before these animals could deliver their sacks of grain.

Horrendous famines in 1906 and 1911 killed 10 million people when floods destroyed farmlands. Fathers sold their daughters for money. The price went down as hunger pangs became unbearable. One father accepted a few coins and two bowls of rice in exchange for his daughter. The food would keep him alive for at least a few days, and he hoped his daughter would be fed by her owner.

[13]

Another frightful famine in 1929 killed over 2 million through starvation, disease, and suicides. Entire families drowned themselves rather than suffer the tortures of slow death.

Periodic famines afflicted China until recently. Although information from mainland China is sketchy and restricted, its government claims that there have been no famines since 1971. Perhaps modern farming methods, improved transportation, and birth control are working miracles in the traditional land of the starving.

INDIA

India has always lived in fear of famine. It is ever at the mercy of monsoons for survival. Monsoons are heavy winds that bring rain in summer and again in winter. They have failed to occur in certain areas so often that a food crisis almost always occurs in some part of India. Most Indians have always lived in extreme poverty. In past centuries a few enjoyed immeasurable wealth and wild extravagances. Rulers sat on thrones of solid gold and ate from jewel-encrusted dishes. Many of these rich rulers were known for their extreme cruelty. During a famine in A.D. 917, although the ground was covered with skeletons, the ruler of Kashmir added to his wealth by selling rice at high prices. Warring rajahs created famines. During the sixteenth century a ruler issued a proclamation forbidding his subjects to farm. Because he wanted to be sure that an invading enemy would not find food, millions of his own people starved to death.

Although many of India's rulers were wicked, others were kind and generous. When a drought-caused famine started to take its toll in 1661, a Mogul emperor opened his treasury and distributed money to his subjects. He also imported corn and gave it away.

One of the worst famines in Indian history occurred in 1770, after three years of drought. Ten million people died of starvation out of a population of 30 million in West Bengal (Bangladesh).

While British officials representing the East India Company ruled India, authorities tried to aid famine-stricken areas. But until rail-links, canals, and good roads were built, little could be done to transport food relief. A British granary, constructed in 1784, has the inscription "For the perpetual prevention of famines in these provinces." Because of poor transportation, the granary was never filled.

In 1812, a plague of locusts destroyed crops. Although food was imported, prices were too high for all but the rich. The governor of Bombay followed the theory of economist Adam Smith: that governments should not interfere with prices set by business. So people died while the economy stayed "healthy."

Ten mammoth famines afflicted India between 1860 and 1900. The Great Famine of 1865, in Orissa, along India's east coast, killed over 10 million. Shiploads of grain were in Calcutta, to be sold in Calcutta. When the authorities finally decided it was proper to interfere with business and ship the grain to Orissa, it was too late. The grain had rotted inside the ships.

In the 1890s the British published its Indian Famine Code, a manual with suggestions for sending aid to starving areas. The Famine Code did save many lives, but it could not keep the ever-present specter of starvation from haunting India.

During World War II, Japanese armies occupying Burma cut off rice exports from Burma to Bengal, northern India. Droves of hunger-crazed Bengalese poured into Calcutta seeking food. Many of them died in the streets, just outside the well-filled, locked storehouses. But food was reserved for factory workers and

**Indian women taking a
course in family planning.**

soldiers, always first to be fed during wartime. More than 5 million died in the Bengal Famine of 1943.

EUROPE

It is hard to believe that for centuries huge famines used to sweep through Europe, destroying entire villages. Before the eighteenth century famines occurred somewhere on the Continent about every ten years. The starving ate dogs and rats. They gnawed on the barks of trees and even swallowed dirt so that their stomachs would feel full. Murderers marketed "two-legged mutton," the cutthroat's term for human flesh. They found willing customers.

Many believed that famines were not due to natural causes but that God was punishing people for their sins. Using their last energies, mobs of wailing penitents dragged themselves through religious processions, praying to heaven for mercy.

Cold weather and heavy rains caused the Great Famine of 1315. In the British Isles and in countries that stretched from the North Sea to the Mediterranean, crops rotted in the fields.

Four wet summers that ruined harvests caused another devastating famine that lasted from 1649 to 1652. Men, women, and children were found dead along Europe's roads.

During the height of Louis XV's glorious reign, France was described as "a vast hospital of dying people." A bishop wrote that "men turned to eating grass like sheep and died like so many flies." Journalists spread false stories that the king was so wicked he made a fortune exporting grain. These stories persisted until the 1790s. It is no wonder that after a series of crop failures between 1783 and 1789 the French Revolution exploded with vicious force.

[17]

As a result of improved agriculture, industry, transportation, and its relatively small population, England was able to escape famine after 1750. But Ireland was doomed to disaster. In 1845, in one terrible month, tiny egg-shaped disease spores carried by the wind turned potato fields into black, stinking heaps of rotting plants.

The potato was Ireland's main food and for most of its people the principal diet. They planted little else.

The potato blight continued for three years. Tenant farmers lost their homes because they were unable to pay rent. They moved their families to holes in the earth, using turf for a roof.

In its efforts to feed the Irish, the British government imported a large shipment of Indian corn from America. But there were scarcely any mills in Ireland that could grind hard corn kernels. Attempts were made to offer relief through public projects, such as road building. But the starving were too weak to work.

At least a million and a half of Ireland's 8 million population starved to death, despite money collected by relief organizations all over the world.

Close to 2 million fled to North America. But most of the ships that took the Irish to Canada and the United States were filthy and unseaworthy. They were called "coffin ships." Some of them disappeared at sea. Those that arrived in America carried passengers dying of disease and starvation. Not all ships were obliged to feed their passengers!

More than other European countries, Russia was cursed by famines that compared in size and horror with those of China and India. The czars ruled over a starving empire of peasants. Some villages survived frequent periods of famine by "hibernating." Massed close together on top of wide stoves, entire families spent winters lying quietly in a semisleep, known as "liojka," only getting up occasionally. In this way they saved energy and needed a minimum of food.

Six major famines afflicted Russia during the last half of the nineteenth century. More were to come in the twentieth century. A famine in 1921, due to the aftereffects of war, revolution, and drought, spread over a million square miles (2½ million square km). Despite the aid of international relief organizations, death claimed 3 million victims.

Soviet land reforms caused one of Russia's worst famines. In 1928 Stalin began to organize state-owned collective farms to increase food production. Farmers were expected to give their land, tools, and animals to the government. In protest, many refused to harvest their grain, and they butchered their animals rather than give them to the State. Civil war broke out, as communist organizers fought farmers. Farmlands were ruined. In 1931 famine gripped the countryside. People in cities also starved. No official figures are available, but estimates of deaths from starvation range from 3 to 10 million people.

With the exception of Russia, no European countries suffered major famines during peacetime after 1900. However, war-caused famines resulted in more deaths than did bombings and battles.

During World War I famines occurred in Russia, Poland, Yugoslavia, Austria, and Germany. Spain suffered food shortages during its Civil War, from 1936 to 1939, when farmlands became battlefields. Although Britain, the United States, and Canada sent aid to Spain, they couldn't prevent a famine that developed by 1938.

During World War II Nazis destroyed enemies by starving them. When they invaded countries they took food away from the people and shipped it to Germany. The Netherlands in 1939 (when some ate tulip bulbs to stay alive) and Greece in 1944 experienced the horrors of famine caused by invaders. Famine also afflicted Russia, where many starved rather than surrender to the Germans. Leningrad endured a nine-hundred-day siege, from September 1941 to January 1944, that resulted in countless deaths from hunger. Nazi "organized hunger" killed fifty thousand Jews walled up in the Warsaw Ghetto from 1940 to 1943, and starvation rations in Nazi concentration camps killed millions of Jews and other so-called undesirables.

Europe has not had a famine since World War II.

MODERN FAMINES

"We are now faced with the fact that tomorrow's today. Over the bleached bones and jumbled residues of numerous civilizations are written the pathetic words: 'Too Late.' "

Martin Luther King, Jr.

We don't have to study past history to learn about famines. We have seen mass starvations on television and have read about them in newspapers and magazines. Photographers bring sad, stirring pictures to us all the way from Asia and Africa. They show us the glazed eyes of men and women lying on the ground waiting for death and the misshapen bodies of children who are too weak to weep.

Children are the main famine victims, because their growing bodies need more protein and calories for their size than do the bodies of adults. *Kwashiorkor* and *marasmus,* children's diseases of malnutrition, are new words in current dictionaries. Kwashiorkor, resulting from insufficient protein, gives children bloated

**This child in Chad is
suffering from kwashiorkor.**

bellies and matchstick arms. Marasmus, caused by too few calories, turns babies into creatures that look like wrinkled old men. Millions of children die from these starvation illnesses. Survivors are often crippled, brain-damaged, or both. During the 1960s and 1970s tragic famines took place in Africa and Asia.

NIGERIA

Famine reaped its harvest of death, mainly among children, during a civil war in Nigeria that lasted from 1967 to 1969.

Government troops blockaded Biafra, a territory fighting to become independent. When supplies of food were cut off, Biafrans lived on a diet of cassava, yams, plantains, and other starchy foods. These foods could not furnish enough protein for growing children. Youngsters died from kwashiorkor.

Supplies could only be brought in by planes landing at night on a small airstrip. Under hostile attack, foreign pilots airlifted protein-rich formula foods and medicines. Despite their heroic deeds, over a million and a half children died from lack of protein. Biafra ceased to exist; it was starved and then conquered by the Nigerian government.

BIHAR, INDIA

Bihar, an Indian state about the size of France, has had a frightful history of famines. Ten million starved to death in 1770, and entire communities have died of hunger since then.

**Grain was finally distributed
in Niger after the civil war.**

In 1965 a drought accompanied by intense heat turned fields into baked clay and wells into dry holes. The people of Bihar feared a great famine similar to those their ancestors had endured.

Although some living in isolated areas starved to death, a mammoth famine was prevented because relief operations were well organized. The United States shipped 18,000,000,000 pounds (8,200,000,000 kg) of wheat. The Indian government arranged for its transportation by rail and road from ports to Bihar.

Fair-price shops were opened where people could purchase food inexpensively. The poor were given free food. Schools became child-care centers where 5 million children and nursing mothers received protein-rich meals. Volunteers of the American Peace Corps and Oxfam (a British organization) dug half a million shallow wells for drinking water.

The rains came in 1968 and the emergency was over. The story of Bihar in 1967 is unique in the history of famine because of the tremendous success of the relief operations. Only thousands died, not millions.

BANGLADESH

The former state of Bengal, India, now Bangladesh, has been a constant disaster zone. It is one of the world's most overcrowded countries, and it has very little industry. In a nation cursed by periodic droughts, floods, locust plagues, and cyclones, most of the people exist in poverty.

Bangladesh suffers from repeated droughts and floods. These people are trying to rebuild irrigation canals to save the land.

In 1971, a civil war in Bangladesh caused famine. Between 9 and 10 million fled south away from famine and fighting into India, toward Calcutta. This sudden exodus from one country to another was the largest ever recorded. A British correspondent said it was as though the entire population of Scotland marched into England for food and housing.

India spent $450 million to set up over a thousand refugee camps, each sheltering from two thousand to fifty thousand Bangladesh refugees.

When the fighting ended in December 1971, and the outlook for crops in Bangladesh looked promising, India, aided by other countries, the United Nations, and volunteer organizations, helped most of the refugees return to their homeland. For many, however, the only choice was another refugee camp in Bangladesh. They returned to misery in their own land.

In 1974 floods covered nearly half of Bangladesh, destroying stored grain and growing crops. The floods were the worst of the century. Women, rarely before seen outside their homes, came into the streets to beg. Those who lived off the beaten track away from roads starved to death.

Even though the floods spoiled enormous quantities of food, there were large quantities of rice that could have been distributed to the hungry. But the government didn't make it available to them. Most of the people were too poor to buy the rice. Therefore, profit-seeking merchants exported it to nearby India, where it sold at high prices.

Bad climate and poverty mean that Bangladesh depends upon help from other countries. This small

Life in a Bangladesh refugee camp is harsh and crowded.

nation of 83 million people, where seven babies are born every minute, can barely exist even in times of peace and normal farming. Bangladesh is always short of food.

THE SAHEL

The Sahel is a strip of land 100 miles (161 km) wide stretching 3,000 miles (4,838 km) across Africa. It borders the southern edge of the Sahara Desert. Sahel means "edge" in Arabic. Six nations exist in this intensely hot, dry area. They are Senegal, Mauritania, Mali, Upper Volta, Niger, and Chad—six of the poorest countries in the world. Ninety percent of their 26 million people are farmers or nomads shepherding livestock, dependent upon rainfall for their survival.

Drought started in 1968. Africans watched their wells dry up, their rivers disappear, and their livestock die. Even Lake Chad, the largest body of water in the region, evaporated and divided into four ponds. The drought also dried up the springs of life for unknown numbers of people.

Nomads whose livelihood depended upon camels, cattle, goats, and sheep lost entire herds. Farmers, who in the best of times tilled poor soil with sharpened sticks, found their land had become barren desert. By the time outside help arrived, 100,000 were dead, and millions had lost their homes and herds.

The rest of the world didn't awaken to the plight of the Sahel until 1972, when the drought was four years old. Then thirty foreign nations sent in food, about half of which came from the United States. The United Nations set up mobile health units to treat the sick and prevent the epidemics that famines usually breed.

**The people of the Sahel watch
cattle die from starvation.**

In some instances, aid was handled so badly by local officials that grain stacked in Western African ports rotted before it could be distributed. Corruption also played its role. For example, trucks with supplies were stopped at the Chad-Nigeria border because the wife of a government official was part owner of a trucking company. She had the supplies transferred to her company's trucks and charged enormous sums to bring food into her own country.

In 1974, after six years of drought, the rains finally came. Then heavy floods in Mali and Niger created new hardships, and a grasshopper plague created further misery. Thousands had to remain in the refugee camps that had been set up through foreign aid. The refugees kept alive by accepting handouts of grain and powdered milk years after the drought had ended. Some, desperate and without hope, committed suicide. When doctors wanted to innoculate children against disease a group of mothers protested. They felt it would be better for their children to die than survive to suffer.

Predictions are frightening. The Sahara Desert is spreading southward at the rate of 30 miles (48 km) each year. It is swallowing the Sahel.

SOMALIA AND ETHIOPIA

In addition to the countries of the Sahel, destructive droughts have afflicted other African nations.

In Somalia, where three-fourths of the people are nomads, a 1974 drought destroyed people and their animals. In 1975 Russia airlifted 120,000 starving no-

The Sahel, here in Upper Volta, is a desolate stretch across Africa.

**Left: this herd of cattle in
Somalia is badly undernourished
and will furnish little food
in return. Above: eighty-five
percent of the cattle in southern
Ethiopia died during the drought.**

mads who had lost their flocks and resettled them on collective farms in the southern part of Somalia and on its coast. This was the largest resettlement of people ever made in Africa. The nomads are being trained to be farmers and fishermen.

In Ethiopia, the rains failed to come in 1970. By 1973, food shortage became famine, killing over one hundred thousand people. Because Emperor Haile Selassie did not want to spoil the tourist trade, he refused to publicize the famine and did not ask for foreign aid. While his people dug mass graves, tourists saw the areas in Ethiopia not affected by drought.

Famine continued until supplies of food and medicine from abroad rescued the country. The famine contributed to Haile Selassie's downfall in 1974. He lost his throne, and the monarchy was abolished.

More help is needed if the people in these countries are to rebuild their lives. Droughts will affect people all over the world. Long-term planning for the future is needed to safeguard people against the tragic, unavoidable periods of bad weather. Only massive international assistance can help save them from future catastrophe.

MIXING
FOOD WITH
POLITICS

"Food is a weapon.
It is now one of the
principal tools in
our negotiating kit."

Earl Butz,
former U.S. Secretary
of Agriculture

he United States has always produced more food than it needed. "Too much" was actually a problem before and after World War II. Farmers couldn't make money because they were growing more than people bought. The government helped by buying and storing surplus grain in warehouses. Old cargo ships found a new use; they were turned into giant storage bins. Huge quantities of food rotted in these floating granaries.

It is hard for us to believe that farmers were paid by the government *not to plant* fields. From the 1930s until 1974 farmers were paid not to cultivate about 50 million acres (20 million hectares) a year. Lands were kept idle to keep grain prices high. Farmers often earned more by growing less. Unfortunately, while fields were deliberately not planted and food was locked away in storage, people all over the world were starving.

After World War II the United States gave away food to countries whose economies had been ruined by the war. Thereafter, it continued giving away food to other needy nations. More than 75 percent of the aid went to governments that opposed communism. South Korea, South Vietnam, and other political allies received bountiful gifts. A mere trickle of grain went to the rest of the hungry world.

As world population grew and the costs of farming went sky-high, the food stockpile shrank. The United States no longer had mountains of surplus grain.

FROM AID TO TRADE

When there was a glut of grain, the United States gave gifts of food. This generosity ended in 1972—a year of crisis. Dry weather destroyed fields in India, Africa, Australia, Argentina, and the Soviet Union. Heavy rains spoiled much of the United States corn and soya bean crops. Aid was cut back. America wanted cash for its crops.

The Soviet Union, formerly a food exporter, became the world's largest grain importer. Because of its crop shortage, it bought one-quarter of the United States wheat crop at bargain prices. It also purchased huge quantities of grain from Canada. By 1973, 60,000,000,000 pounds (27,000,000,000 kg) of grain left North America for the Soviet Union. This was the largest sale of food in history. The enormous grain deliveries weren't needed to ward off famine. A large portion was used to feed Russian livestock.

Because of the Russian grain drain, prices of meat and animal feed skyrocketed all over the world. The cost of bread was higher in the United States than in Russia. Transportation was a mess. American rail boxcars, clogged with Russian-bought wheat, had little

space for other products. Ships loading grain destined for Russia jammed ports. At the same time, famines were killing people in India, Bangladesh, and the African Sahel.

The world food crisis became still worse in 1973 when the Arab oil-producing nations shocked the world with an oil embargo. Oil prices quadrupled. When the price of oil goes up, the price of many things needed to grow food goes up, too. Fuel used for tractors, irrigation pumps, and harvesters became very expensive. Because the production of fertilizers requires large amounts of oil, the fertilizer supply dwindled and prices zoomed. Farm production dropped in poor countries unable to afford oil products. They had to look to North America for help.

The prices of wheat and rice tripled from 1972 to 1974. During its ghastly famine, Bangladesh could not afford to pay for a large shipment of wheat it had contracted to buy. It had to cancel its order in July 1974. The United States government finally sent aid. Food reached Bangladesh in time for Christmas 1974—after the worst of the famine was over. So much food poured in that Bangladesh didn't have enough storage space. Rats grew fat on delayed United States charity.

After a poor harvest in 1975, the Soviet Union once again purchased huge amounts of American wheat. The United States was accused of "grain diplomacy." By feeding Russians Secretary of State Kissinger could arrange friendly talks about peace in the Middle East. During these talks, Syria, too, received United States food. Full stomachs made talks more pleasant.

**American emergency aid arrives
in Dakar in West Africa.**

Food has been used as a political weapon, denied to unpopular governments and offered to nations whose welfare is important to our view of world security. The United States has sent enormous quantities of rice to its ally South Korea. It has shipped rice to Indonesia and wheat to Venezuela; both are able to supply oil in return. Food at reasonable prices can decide whether or not a government will survive. For example, the United States refused to sell food to Chile when its president was procommunist Salvadore Allende. Food shortages were one reason for his downfall. After he was ousted, American grain poured into Chile.

Because the United States is the world's greatest food exporter, it has life-and-death power over millions of people all over the world. Should there be a global food shortage, the United States may have to decide who eats and who starves.

How much moral responsibility does a rich country have for feeding poor nations? Should it increase food aid even if it means increasing food prices at home? Over 16 million Americans go to bed hungry every night. While their own welfare rolls are increasing, are Americans supposed to sacrifice to help people on the other side of the globe? There are no easy answers.

LIFEBOAT ETHICS

Today, in a world of starving millions, Americans are facing serious moral problems. If there really isn't enough food to go around, how does the government decide who shall be fed?

The United States grain sorghum was airlifted to drought-stricken Nigeria.

WFP PRO NO. 979
TA-3050-1
GRAIN SORGHUM
UNITED STATES OF AMERICA
PEOPLE

Some scientists recommend "lifeboat ethics," a theory first proposed by Garrett Hardin, a California biologist. The rich, he wrote, are adrift in lifeboats in a sea of hunger. Survivors in crowded lifeboats are justified in beating back all who try to climb aboard. "In the ocean outside each lifeboat swim the poor of the world who would like to get in, or at least share some of the wealth. What should the lifeboat passengers do? We could try to take everyone aboard, but we would sink in the lifeboat if we did. The boat swamps, everyone drowns."

Kenneth Boulding, an economist from the University of Colorado, has also written about the futility of saving the hopelessly poor: ". . . it permits a larger proportion to live in precisely the same state of misery and starvation."

Is it better to put the poor out of their misery by allowing them to die?

Triage is a blood-chilling idea recommended by some food experts. A French word, it is the name of the system used in military medicine for sorting the wounded into three groups: those who would survive without medicine; the "hopeless cases" who would probably die despite the best care; and those who would live if they received medical help. Medical attention was limited to the third group. The "hopeless cases" were left to die.

Today the theory of triage could be applied by rich nations with limited food supplies. Nations, like wounded soldiers, are divided into three groups: those who would survive without food aid; the "hopeless cases"—feeding them just keeps them alive longer and prolongs their agony; and nations that would help themselves after they received aid.

William and Paul Paddock spoke about triage in

their book, *Time of Famines.* "Call triage cold-blooded," they say, "but it is derived from the hard experience of humaneness during a crisis. Waste not the food on the 'can't be saved.' "

Many feel that brutal and cruel decisions will have to be made. They argue that since the United States does not have enough to feed the entire world, it should help only those nations that will help themselves. Poor countries that need aid must show they are trying to put their own houses in order. Many scientists insist that governments wanting aid must plan birth control campaigns and invest their own money in farm reforms.

Must the rich nations make heartless choices? Instead of comparing the world to a battlefield or to a lifeboat, some writers describe our planet as a badly run ocean liner. First-class passengers devour mammoth steaks and guzzle all the grain whiskey they want. Mobs below deck barely have enough to eat. If those on top refuse to share, the hungry will eventually rush up from their crowded, miserable quarters, use violence, and take over the ship.

The rich may be *forced* to become moral. The situation becomes more critical as poorer nations invest in weapons. Too many countries own more weapons than farm machinery. They arm well rather than farm well. Instead of spending large amounts of money for land reform, India paid billions to develop its own nuclear bombs. Other poor nations will, undoubtedly, have atomic weapons in the future. If food keeps being hogged by the rich, poor nations may threaten to use force if they are not well fed.

Rich nations, for purely selfish reasons, would do best to help the world with food and with technical assistance.

CAN SCIENCE
SAVE US?

"... whoever could make two ears
of corn, or two blades of grass
to grow upon a spot of ground
where only one grew before, would
deserve the better of mankind,
and do more essential service to
his country, than the whole race
of politicians put together."

Jonathan Swift

Unless the world triples its food production by the year 2000, there may be massive famines. More foods and new foods must be taken from the soil and the sea.

NEW FOODS

In the 1950s scientists succeeded in breeding new types of wheat, corn, and rice. In Mexico a new "miracle wheat" yielded twice as much grain as before. In the Philippines a "miracle rice," called IR-8, grew like magic in the soil, producing four to ten times more rice than ever before. High-yield seeds were sent in bulk to poor nations. By 1973 over 80 million acres (32 million hectares) in Asia and North Africa were growing the miracle plants. A new era in agriculture was proclaimed. It was called the *Green Revolution.*

IR-8-288-3, a variation
of "miracle rice."

The Green Revolution was hailed as the answer to the global food problem. Breeding new varieties of seeds that brought in larger harvests seemed to have unlimited possibilities. If scientists could continue creating new, hardy crops, then the poorest countries might be able to grow enough food for their own people.

But the Green Revolution started to look sickly yellow after 1973. The new seeds had to be fed large quantities of fertilizer, pesticides, and water. When the prices of fuel, fertilizers, and pesticides went up, miracle crops drooped.

The Green Revolution needed money most farmers didn't have. They couldn't afford to pay for the fuel that irrigation pumps require or the tractors and chemicals needed for big harvests. The miracle crops were best suited to big business agriculture (agribusiness). To make matters worse, when the big farms flooded the market with enormous quantities of grain, its price went down. As a result, many farmers were unable to eke out a living from their small plots of land. They sold their farms to the big companies. Big farms benefited; small ones suffered. The Green Revolution left some people worse off than ever before.

Dr. Norman E. Borlaug, the leading scientist of the Green Revolution, declared that governments were just going to have to distribute seeds, fertilizers, and pesticides free of charge. Water pumps would have to be installed and irrigation channels built for all. "If we can't get the Green Revolution to the little guy, there is no revolution," he said.

Researchers are developing new seeds that need less fertilizer, fewer pesticides, and less water. In 1975 three new strains of grain were developed. New, improved seeds resistant to most pests and diseases are being distributed at low prices to small farms.

MORE LAND

Even if farmlands succeed in growing bigger and better crops, there may not be enough good land left on earth for growing more food. About 3,600,000,000 acres (1,440,000,000 hectares) of the earth are cultivated. Some claim there isn't much more land left suitable for crops; others insist that at least 6,600,000,000 more acres (2,640,000,000 hectares) could be planted.

The search for new lands has resulted in proposed projects that sound impossible and improbable. Scientists have been eyeing jungles, deserts, and frozen wastelands.

Dense growths, drenching rains, and blistering heat have ruled out jungle farming in the past. However, bulldozers could clear jungles, build terraces for holding soil, and dig irrigation channels to regulate the amount of water fed to plants. Fertilizers could be applied to enrich soils lacking minerals that have been washed away by driving rainfalls. In this way, vast areas could be farmed in the Amazon Basin of Brazil and in the Mekong Delta of Vietnam and Cambodia.

Africa has over 2 million square miles (5.18 million square km) of promising land. The tsetse fly, carrier of sleeping sickness, keeps farmers and cattle growers away. Time and money could make this land safe from disease. Experts say that within ten years, at a cost of $1,000,000,000, the tsetse fly could be eliminated from Africa.

What about desert and semidesert, which cover about one-third of the world's surface? Fourteen million acres (5.6 million hectares) a year die as sands cover good earth. Desert lands are increasing as trees are cut down and the ground is overfarmed and overgrazed. Some experts predict that at the rate deserts are taking over, half the land now farmed could become barren by the year 2000. Scientists must not only halt this growth but also transform deserts into farmlands.

Israel has succeeded in making its desert bloom. Experts are performing miracles in the land of the Bible. Fruit orchards flourish in the middle of the Negev, Israel's moonscape desert. Pipelines bring water long distances from the Sea of Galilee. In addition to water, expert farming techniques coax food from once-barren land.

Frozen wastelands could disappear with twenty-first-century advances. Scattering coal dust could be used to melt snow, and by using giant heaters and super-strong lights, icy areas of our planet could become green fields.

The problem of finding more land has resulted in many imaginative proposals. Greenhouse farming has been suggested for cities and suburbs of industrial countries. Glass-enclosed farms would produce enough food for built-up communities. Greenhouse farming could make up for the terrible loss of valuable farmland caused when roads, shopping areas, and housing developments are built.

Greenhouses are using hydroponics, the technique of growing food without using soil. Plastic- or concrete-lined beds are filled with foam plastic, granite, sand, or just a solution of water and fertilizer. Seedlings planted in these beds grow with their roots nourished by water and plant food. Many vegetables, such as tomatoes and cucumbers, are grown this way.

**Hydroponic cultivation
of substitute protein.**

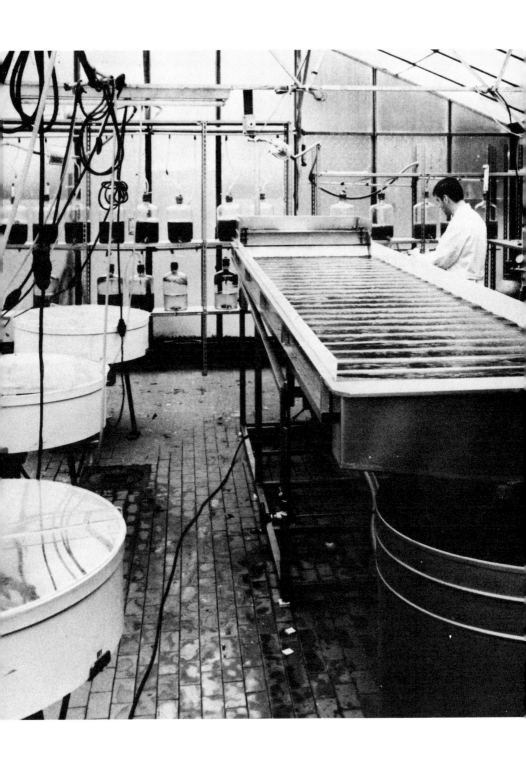

Farming without soil takes place not only in greenhouses, but out-of-doors, in areas where the soil is poor. Scientists have schemes for growing soil-free vegetable gardens underground and on farm satellites orbiting in outer space.

Scientists have the know-how. One problem is cost. Doubling world food production by using more land and newer plants would require more than $1,000,000,000,000. Lester Brown, an expert on food problems, has said, "The people who are talking about adding more land are not considering the cost. If you are willing to pay the price, you can farm the slopes of Mt. Everest."

Some of the price paid can't be measured just in terms of money. Too much of our earth's natural beauty has already been destroyed by asphalt and concrete used to build highways and cities. Wild creatures, robbed of their wilderness homes, are dying. Many have been poisoned by pesticides that can damage the soil and affect the health of animals and people who eat food grown in that soil. In many areas dangerous levels of poison have been found in mothers' milk, cows' milk, beef, pigs, and poultry. Pesticides wash out of the soil into streams, lakes, rivers, and oceans, where they pollute the waters and can kill fish. By saturating the ground with chemicals we risk destroying important foods.

MORE WATER

New sources of water are also hard to find. About three out of four people don't have water fit for drinking or for irrigating land. The shortage of water, rather than the shortage of land, may be the main threat to future survival. The United Nations Food and Agriculture Organization has stated that because of increased population and growing industry, the world will require twice as much fresh water by the year 2000 as is used today.

Of the world's fresh water supply, less than 1 percent is usable. Most of the planet's usable water is locked in glaciers and polar ice caps.

Plans are now under way to hitch tugs to icebergs and haul them to distant lands. The Iceberg Transportation Company, a Saudi Arabian firm formed in 1977, has a $100 million proposal: hauling a 200-million-pound (91-million-kg) iceberg 6,000 miles (9,677 km), from Antarctica to the coast of Saudi Arabia. Bringing icebergs to Arabia sounds like bringing the mountain to Mohammed.

Changing the direction of rivers is another science scheme. A few years ago the Soviet Union planned to reverse the flow of four rivers that empty into the Arctic Ocean. They would do this by using atomic explosions to make dams and canals. Instead of spilling into the ocean, fresh water would then be able to irrigate fields. After loud protests from ecologists, the Soviets shelved this grand scheme. However, they are building a 175-mile (281-km) canal that will change the direction of some of the waters of two rivers.

The Australian Snowy Mountains Scheme, one of the world's largest irrigation and power projects, can provide water for at least 1,000 square miles (2,600 square km) of land. Tunnels, dams, aqueducts, and power stations built from 1949 to 1974 changed the course of three major rivers. Instead of emptying into the sea, waters directed inland transformed dry fields into fertile farms.

Other large bodies of water exist underground, even underneath deserts. A company engaged to drill

for oil found a buried lake 160 miles (258 km) long and 180 miles (290 km) wide beneath the scorching Sahara.

Some claim that tapping Egypt's underground lake would have been cheaper and better than building the Aswan High Dam. Although the famous dam irrigates a huge area, it cuts off the Nile's fertile mud deposits. Artificial fertilizers must be used, at costs a poor nation can ill afford. The waters of the dam also spread bilharzia, a disabling disease caused by snails that thrive in the waters of the Nile. The waters are stored and channeled to farms by the Aswan Dam.

As the need for water becomes more critical, increasing attention is given to oceans. Desalinization, removing salt from seawater, is used in the United States, Saudi Arabia, Mexico, and in many other countries.

Rainmaking, seeding certain types of clouds with chemicals, is another expensive way of producing water. But tampering with weather has brought storms of protest. In 1973, when Rhodesia seeded clouds, the poorer, adjacent nations accused it of stealing rain from them. In 1977 Idaho accused the state of Washington of "cloud rustling," declaring that by seeding clouds it was grabbing rain that could have drifted to Idaho.

Pipelines, wells, huge dams, and canals irrigate about one-tenth of the world's farms. That's a drop in the earth's bucket. Most farm families have no irrigation, no cash, no credit, and no hope for much needed water.

A recent Japanese study states that proper irrigation could double rice production in Asia within fifteen

Ten-year-old Khelon helps rebuild an irrigation canal in Bangladesh.

years. But as energy costs mount, poor nations are not investing in large-scale irrigation.

FARMING THE SEA

The sea has always been considered a constant, limitless source of food. Many have looked to the oceans for the answer to the population-food problem.

The global fish catch increased at the rate of 5 percent a year from 1945 to 1970. People expected that it would keep increasing as more and more fleets were built and mammoth nets dragged the oceans. But in the 1970s there was a dramatic drop in the amount of fish caught. Anchovies, which had always been plentiful off the Peruvian coastline, became scarce. Catches of North Sea herring, Atlantic haddock and cod, and Pacific sardines dwindled. Many other types of fish disappeared completely.

Overfishing had been destroying ocean life. Instead of increasing the world's supply, modern fleets were killing food sources.

The destruction goes on now. Fleets are equipped with electric fish finders, nets that stretch for miles, and pumps that pull fish out of the nets with incredible speed. Spotter planes are sometimes used to detect schools of fish, and fast motorboats herd fish into waiting nets. Underwater lights attract fish to the surface, and air bubbles pumped down to the ocean floor also bring fish to the top. Huge factory ships, remaining at sea for months at a time, are capable of hauling in fish at the rate of 500,000 pounds (227,273 kg) a day.

Fish ponds in Africa are used to train fishermen as well as provide food.

Pollution has also been spoiling the ocean's harvest. Rivers of oil are spilled each year and the chances are that this amount will increase. Industrial plants, using rivers and oceans as their sewers, continue to poison fish. Jacques Cousteau, the French underwater explorer, estimates that marine life has declined 80 percent since 1945 because of pollution and overfishing.

The search is on for new kinds of fish to make up for the shortage of many popular varieties. Large quantities of so-called "trash fish," thrown back to sea, could be used as nourishing food. Species like shark, skate, and squid should find wider acceptance at the dinner table. Fish biologists point out that there are about forty thousand kinds of sea life; people have tasted a thousand at most.

Russians and Japanese have been eating *krill,* a tiny shrimplike creature found in huge masses in the Antarctic. Krill is made into a fish paste, not very delicious, but very rich in protein. Krill is also used as a fertilizer. The disturbing problem is that krill is a food for other sea life. Should krill be overfished, Antarctic whales, seals, and many fish might starve.

People in Thailand eat *plankton.* Plankton, made up of small plants (algae) and tiny animals, drift with the ocean's currents. In 1947 when the Norwegian Thor Heyerdahl crossed the Pacific Ocean on his famous raft, *Kon-Tiki,* he and his crew of five caught, ate, and enjoyed plankton every day.

Fish farming is another way of increasing the amount of food. In Asia fish are bred and fed in the ditches of rice fields. Usually, fish are farmed in ponds.

Carp ponds in Israel are yielding substantial amounts of protein-rich fish each year. African countries are raising tilapia, a perchlike fish that grows quickly and breeds plentifully. Thailand has been farming catfish in large quantities. Raising trout and catfish in ponds is a big business in the United States.

Offshore harvests are also being reaped. Giant prawns are cultivated in Malaysian waters, and oysters and mussels are grown off the coast of Spain.

Despite high yields, production costs limit fish farming. At best, it cannot begin to equal the riches the oceans hold.

FOOD FROM FACTORIES

Modern day alchemists are transforming crude oil, waste rubber, newspapers, garbage, sewage, and weeds into food.

Factories are changing petroleum into a protein called SCP, or Single Cell Protein. It is being used to feed livestock, but further refinements may bring oil-based foods straight to the dinner table. SCP needs neither soil nor sunshine. It is grown and harvested indoors on waxes made from oil. A 250-acre (101-hectare) factory could make as much protein as a million acres of soya beans.

FPC, Fish Protein Concentrate, is a flour made from whole fish, including scales, bones, and guts. It is sold, and in many cases given free to poor people, who use it for baking bread, thickening soups and stews, and making desserts.

Grasses and weeds have also been made into acceptable dishes after the parts that cannot be digested are removed.

Formulas in liquid and powder form are being mass-produced by big corporations and shipped to poor countries. They are high-calorie, protein-rich

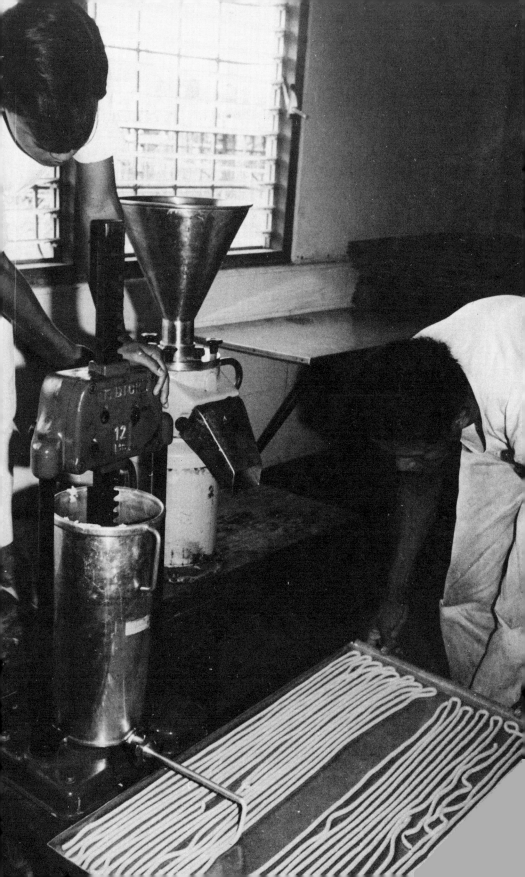

food supplements. Government and relief agencies distribute them to the poor. They may cure the high death-rates among preschool children. In many poor countries one child in five dies before reaching the fifth birthday because of diseases caused by protein deficiency.

Even rich countries are using factory-made foods. Inflation has forced people to acquire a taste for imitation meats. Supermarkets sell fake bacon, beef, pork, and turkey. These "meats" are made from soya beans that machines spin and shape into chops, roasts, and hamburgers.

Rubbish, garbage, and sewage are being used to make animal feed. When chemically treated, they grow algae, the same nourishing plants found in plankton. At the American General Electric Company, cow manure, treated with bacteria, turns into a mass that is dried into a powder with a high protein content. Food from waste materials are only for animals. Grain, instead of being used for cows and pigs, could then be available for the world's hungry people.

Farm plants make up the bulk of the world diet. Factory foods are an expensive, tasteless substitute for the products from land and sea.

Meanwhile, babies are coming faster than bread can be baked.

**Pasta made from beans provides
high protein at low cost.**

THE RACE
AGAINST FAMINE

**"Morally it makes no difference
whether a man is killed in war or
is condemned to starve to death
by the indifference of others."**

**Willy Brandt
Former West German Chancellor**

Despite great strides in science, the causes of famine are still with us. Famines from droughts and floods constantly occur somewhere in the world. Although scientists can breed miracle plants, find more water, develop new land, and produce better fertilizers, they are still baffled by the whims of weather. Climate cannot be controlled. When rains fail, freezing winds blow, or a scorching sun bakes soil into clay, people starve to death.

Although their forecasts differ, many climatologists feel that the earth is about to undergo drastic changes in weather patterns. A United States government study warns that "a new climatic era brings promise of famine and starvation to many areas of the world."

According to Dr. Reid Bryson, Director of the Institute for Environmental Studies, the world has been getting colder since about 1950. We could be entering a new ice age. Eventually glaciers descending from the Arctic will cover much of Europe, Canada, and the northern third of the United States. Although the new ice age will take thousands of years to develop devastating glaciers, a gradual cooling trend will soon affect the amount and kind of food that can be grown.

Within the next twenty years, our planet may become 1°C (1.8°F) cooler. This would shorten the frost-free period in New England and Canada by about twelve days. As a result, one-third of Canada's wheat acreage would be spoiled. The one degree cooling would chill the heart of Florida's orange area, greatly increasing the chance of frost killing the citrus harvest. The drop in temperature is an immediate problem. "It is something that if it continues will affect the whole human occupation of the earth—like 1,000,000,000 starving people," Dr. Bryson warns.

Some climatologists disagree with Dr. Bryson. They predict that the world will get warmer. But their forecasts hold no greater promise for the future. Warmer weather could produce more storms and more devastating floods.

Someday scientists may be able to change the climate of the earth. But current forecasts are gray and chilling. Climate-food disasters lie ahead, even if we are not on the threshold of an ice age.

THE NEED FOR A
WORLD GRANARY

There is an urgent need for a world granary. Foodstuffs must be stocked and stored through international cooperation. Stockpiling must begin at once, not because we know what climate is going to do, but because we don't know.

Food from an internationally run granary could prevent famines. Reserves would consist largely of grains, because these can be stored and transported more easily than other foods.

Many conferences have plotted plans for food reserves. The World Food Conference of 1974 resulted in many elaborate speeches. The aim of the Conference was stated: "Every man, woman, and child has the inalienable right to be free from hunger."

Although a resolution was passed that stocks and funds from rich countries be earmarked for emergencies anywhere on earth, results were shocking. Nations wrangled among themselves about how much money each was to contribute. The issue was not how to help the hungry but how much each country was expected to give. No agreement was signed.

The United Nations World Food Council, which met in 1977, echoed the lofty aims of 1974: hunger was to be eliminated from the earth. Once again, there was much talk and little action. The rich countries would not agree to stockpile grain in amounts needed by the poorer nations. They feared that large grain surpluses would push farm prices down.

The World Food Council warned that by the mid 1980s, 43 countries could be short of more than 200,000,000,000 pounds (91,000,000,000 kg) of grain, even if there were no major crop disasters. Nevertheless, rich nations have been dragging their feet and eyeing each other to make sure the burden will be divided fairly. A committee chosen by the World Food Council is expected to offer a plan to the United Nations

Malnourishment will continue
in Chad, and elsewhere, if
answers for famine are not found.

General Assembly after June 1978. Assuming that the international political climate continues to cloud the issues, there may be years of discussion. By that time there may not be any surplus stock to argue about.

FAIR WEATHER PROBLEMS

Good weather brought record harvests to the United States and Canada in 1976 and 1977. The Soviet Union, North America's best customer, had no need to buy shiploads of wheat, for it, too, enjoyed bumper crops.

Surpluses became a problem for the American farmer. Prices of grain dropped to two dollars a bushel, half the price of 1975. Because the costs of fertilizers and machinery continued to rise, farmers faced tremendous losses.

In order to help farmers earn a living, President Carter proposed that 20 percent of all wheat acreage be kept idle. That meant 11 million acres (4.5 million hectares) would not be planted—land that could grow 40,000,000,000 pounds (18,000,000,000 kg) of wheat! Only those farmers who kept a portion of their fields fallow would receive government aid. As in the years between 1930 and 1974, farmers, once again, would be paid *not* to plant. President Carter also proposed setting aside 12,000,000,000 pounds (5,400,000,000 kg) of grain for an International Emergency Food Reserve.

The problem is complex. The world needs as much surplus grain as it can stock. (At the time the president made these proposals, famine was killing villagers in Ghana and in West Africa.) However, if prices are allowed to drop due to overproduction, how will the farmer make ends meet?

The United States has been called "the bread-basket of the world." Although it makes up less than 6 percent of the global population, its farmers feed

one-quarter of the world. One American farmer grows enough for forty-five people.

American farmers can't be expected to pay the world's dinner bills by selling their produce at a loss. If farms are forced to close down, there will be less food than ever for hungry nations. Food reserves must be worked out by all nations on a fair-share basis.

THE SPECTER OF FAMINE

A world granary doesn't solve the food shortage. It is an emergency food bank that helps in times of crisis. Even if granaries are filled we must be sure that disaster areas have trucks and decent roads for distributing food. Good storage is also needed. Rot, rats, and insects now destroy over half the foods in most poor countries.

Not only food, but funds must be sent from the well-fed to the hungry. Money must be spent for dams, irrigation canals, fertilizer plants, and research stations. Farmers must be given money or be able to borrow it on easy terms for new tools and better seeds. The most urgent task is helping the poor improve their overall economy and their agriculture.

True aid follows the proverb, "If you give me fish I will eat today; if you teach me to fish, I will eat for the rest of my life." Rich nations must send out scientists and instructors to teach people how best to use their lands. The United Nations, many governments, and private organizations are helping the needy. But their funds are too limited, and they improve the plight of relatively few.

Eighty million extra mouths to feed each year! The earth has limited space for producing food and housing people.

Visionaries predict that a hundred years from now new worlds will be conquered and occupied. Floating communities will be launched into outer space, and millions will migrate from Earth to clean cities and green fields on human-made satellites. Perhaps cities will float on oceans, and thrive underground—even under the sea. These would house the surplus population that has crowded and polluted the planet Earth.

Before these dreams could possibly come true, famines could kill.

BIBLIOGRAPHY

Aykroyd, W. R. *The Conquest of Famine.* Pleasant-ville, N.Y.: Reader's Digest, 1975.

Borgstrom, Georg. *Focal Points.* New York: Macmillan, 1973.

————. *The Hungry Planet.* New York: Macmillan, 1967.

————. *World Food Resources.* New York: Intext Educational Publishers, 1973.

Brown, Lester R. *Seeds of Change: The Green Revolution & Development in the 1970's.* New York: Praeger, 1970.

Brown, Lester, and Eckholm, Erik. *By Bread Alone.* New York: Praeger, 1974.

Ehrlich, Paul. *The Population Bomb.* New York: Ballantine, 1971.

George, Susan. *How the Other Half Dies.* London: Penguin, 1976.

Halacy, D. S., Jr. *The Geometry of Hunger.* New York: Harper & Row, 1972.

Kahn, Herman. *The Next 2000 Years.* New York: Morrow, 1976.

Lappe, Francis. *Diet for a Small Planet.* New York: Ballantine, 1971.

Lappe, Francis, and Collins, Joseph. *Food First.* Boston: Houghton Mifflin, 1977.

Marx, Herbert L., Jr., ed. *The World Food Crisis.* New York: Wilson, 1975.

National Research Council. *World Food & Nutrition Study.* Washington, D.C.: National Academy of Sciences, 1977.

Paddock, William, and Paddock, Paul. *Time of Famines.* Boston: Little Brown, 1976.

Schneider, Stephen H., and Mesiorw, Lynne E. *The Genesis Strategy.* New York: Plenum Publishing, 1976.

Stamp, Elizabeth, ed. *Growing Out of Poverty.* Oxford: Oxford University Press, 1977.

Trager, James. *Amber Waves of Grain.* New York: Arthur Field Books, 1973.

U.S. Department of Agriculture. *The World Food Situation and Prospects to 1985.* Washington, D.C.: U.S. Department of Agriculture, 1975.

Vicker, Ray. *This Hungry World.* New York: Scribner's, 1975.

Woodham-Smith, Cecil B. *The Great Hunger.* New York: Harper & Row, 1963.

FURTHER READING

Bernarde, Melvin. *Race Against Famine.* Philadelphia: Macrae Smith, 1968.

Chadwick, Lee. *Seeds of Plenty.* New York: Coward-McCann, 1969.

Halacy, D. S., Jr. *Feast and Famine.* Philadelphia: Macrae Smith, 1971.

Perl, Lila. *The Global Food Shortage.* New York: Morrow, 1976.

Pringle, Laurence. *Our Hungry Earth.* New York: Macmillan, 1976.

Raskin, Edith. *World Food.* New York: McGraw-Hill, 1971.

Scott, John. *Hunger.* New York: Parents Magazine, 1969.

ORGANIZATIONS

The following organizations can supply materials relating to the world food crisis:

Agency for International Development
Office of Public Affairs
State Department Building
Washington, D.C. 20523

Christian Aid
2 Sloane Gardens
London, SW1, England

The U.S. Department of Agriculture
Independence Avenue at 14th Street, S.W.
Washington, D.C. 20250

Environmental Protection Agency
Public Affairs Office
Public Inquiries
Rockville, Md. 20852

The U.S. Department of
Health, Education and Welfare
330 Independence Avenue, S.W.
Washington, D.C. 20201

International Planned Parenthood Federation
515 Madison Avenue
New York, N.Y. 10022
Nutrition Foundation
99 Park Avenue
New York, N.Y. 10016

Oxfam America
302 Columbus Avenue
Boston, Mass. 02116

Oxfam (England)
274 Banbury Road
Oxford, England

Population Crisis Committee
1730 K. Street, N.W.
Washington, D.C. 20006

Population Reference Bureau, Inc.
1754 N. Street, N.W.
Washington, D.C. 20036

Resources for the Future, Inc.
1755 Massachusetts Avenue, N.W.
Washington, D.C. 20036

United Nations
Office of Public Information
New York, N.Y. 10017

War on Want
476 Calendonian Road
London, N7, England

Organizations in Canada

Canadian Save the Children Fund (CANSAVE)
70 Hayter Street
Toronto, Ontario M5G 1J6

Oxfam Canada
251 Laurier Ave. W.
Ottawa, Ontario K1P 5J6

Oxfam Quebec
169 East Rue Saint Paul
Montreal, Quebec H2Y 1G8

UNICEF Canada
443 Mt. Pleasant Road
Toronto, Ontario M4S 2L8

Unitarian Service Committee
56 Sparks Street
Ottawa, Ontario K1P 5B1

INDEX

[80]

[81]

ABOUT
THE AUTHOR

In the course of her varied writing career, Rhoda Blumberg has written for radio and magazines, and published a number of books for both adults and children. For Franklin Watts, Ms. Blumberg has authored *Firefighters, Sharks, UFO,* and *First Ladies,* all First Books.

Rhoda Blumberg travels a great deal but still manages to enjoy her home overlooking the hills of Yorktown Heights, New York, where, in addition to writing, she raises horses, swims, plays tennis, and leads a local youth group.